The Humility
of the Brutes

Southern Messenger Poets

Dave Smith, Series Editor

The Humility of the Brutes

Poems

RON SMITH

LOUISIANA STATE UNIVERSITY PRESS   BATON ROUGE

Published by Louisiana State University Press
Manufactured in the United States of America
LSU Press Paperback Original
First printing

Photograph on book cover by Ron Smith.
The author thanks Sari Gilbert for help securing permissions.

Designer: Laura Roubique Gleason
Typefaces: Display: Albertan L; Text: Miller Text
Printer and binder: LSI

Library of Congress Cataloging-in-Publication Data

Names: Smith, Ron, 1949 February 12–, author.
Title: The humility of the brutes : poems / Ron Smith.
Description: Baton Rouge : Louisiana State University Press, [2017]
Identifiers: LCCN 2017005116 | ISBN 978-0-8071-6656-7 (pbk. : alk. paper) |
ISBN 978-0-8071-6657-4 (pdf) | ISBN 978-0-8071-6658-1 (epub)
Classification: LCC PS3569.M537963 A6 2017 | DDC 811/.54—dc23
LC record available at https://lccn.loc.gov/2017005116

for

Delores and Brooks

love and humility
(and occasional lightning)

I think that we who are poets and artists, not being permitted to shoot beyond the tangible, must go from desire to weariness and so to desire again, and live but for the moment when vision comes to our weariness like terrible lightning, in the humility of the brutes.

—William Butler Yeats, *Per Amica Silentia Lunae*

Contents

Acknowledgments

I am grateful to the editors of the following periodicals and anthologies, in which these poems first appeared. Some poems have been revised since their first appearance, and some titles have changed.

Aethlon: "Edgar Athletic Poe," "Hurdling the Wedge," "Monk & Mason," "Thirteen Ways of Looking at Half-Rubber," "What's Wrong with the Baseball Hall of Fame," and "What's Right with the Baseball Hall of Fame"; *Anglican Theological Review:* "Birds of the Air"; *Arete:* "Noseguard"; *Artemis:* "Virgin & Child with Monkey"; *Blackbird:* "A foolish moon in a foolish sky" and "St. Petersburg, Petrograd, Leningrad, Petersburg"; *Broad Street:* "1911," "After Church," "Angelus: Chesapeake Bay," and "John Smith in Virginia"; *College English:* "The Old Crabber Has Gone Deaf"; *CrossRoads:* "That Coach in My Head Never Stops Asking How Much I Want It"; *Encore:* "Vandalism of the Library Door"; *Great Stream Review:* "Boot Hill & the Alimentary Spirit World of Southern Joy"; *Hampden-Sydney Poetry Review:* "Cairbre & Bres the Beautiful" and "The Good People"; *Make It New:* "Apocalypse," "Erice," "Eternal," "Leningrad," and "Seven Years After the Fall"; *The Mind of Monticello: Fifty Contemporary Poets on Jefferson:* "Mr. Jefferson Speaks of Rapture"; *Puerto del Sol:* "Bronze Boxer"; *Plume:* "Coda alla Vaccinara," "A Dusting," "Work: Savannah Roots," and "Winkles & Dillisk"; *The Plume Anthology of Poetry:* "Forum Boarium," "Maximus, Minimus," and "De Danaans, or Thank God for Plastic"; *Poetry Northwest:* "Jacob, Swinging"; *Poultry: A Magazine of Voice:* "Oh, Duh! to the Confederate Dead"; *Remapping Richmond's Hallowed Ground:* "Artificer"; *Shenandoah:* "What a Rush"; *Southern Poetry Review:* "Brampton Road" and "Ultima Thule"; *Terminus:* "Barelli Calls," "The Birth of Modern Poetry," and "Just the Big Three."

Thanks also to the editors of periodicals, anthologies, and online sites where some of the above poems have been reprinted.

Broadside: The Magazine of the Library of Virginia: "Mr. Jefferson Speaks of Rapture"; *A Common Wealth of Poetry:* "Brampton Road";

The Huffington Post: "The Old Crabber Has Gone Deaf"; *Jet Fuel:* "Caibre & Bres the Beautiful"; *Kentucky: Poets of Place:* "Oh, Duh! to the Confederate Dead"; *Make It New:* "The Birth of Modern Poetry"; *Moving Boys Forward:* "1911" and "Monk & Mason"; *Poetry Daily:* "Cairbre & Bres the Beautiful," "What a Rush," and "St. Petersburg, Petrograd, Leningrad, Petersburg."

The Humility
of the Brutes

A Dusting

The sun was the moon all morning,
the trees signatures of trees. Where

had you been, emptiness, my old friend?

Nary a cow, a single crater—white hole
in the luminous gray.
                    I crossed the field, I re-
crossed the field. A dusting, as we say.

Footprints: waves, wavelengths:

A human being can't go straight. I turn,
I begin.
            Which is to say, I begin again.

Bronze Boxer

first century B.C.

Battered, not butchered, to make a Roman
holiday, this fellow's not thinking of
a rude hut anywhere, but that contusion
below his right eye, its throb, and above
both brows the stinging from astringent applied
by his old coach, a man he loves, for this
life he lives, this agon and fame, the pride
he carries down the dungy street, the kiss
the best courtesan eagerly bestows
at the quietest place in the Subura.
Wrung out, bleeding, dignified, he knows
whoever that is calling him is a
fan, not a friend, thinks, *Check the other guy.*
I bet he's still there, looking at the sky.

Mr. Jefferson Speaks of Rapture

Natural Bridge, Virginia

Even though he knows Cedar Creek
pours through it, he wants to believe
    it was cloven by a great convulsion.
        Master of all he surveys, he's
been measuring it from below for some time. This,
    he will say, must not be
    pretermitted. God's Roman arch,
he will not say, not this empire hater. He always
        provides a number of numbers.

        "The arch approaches
the semi-elliptical form; but the larger axis
of the ellipsis, which would be the cord
of the arch, is many times longer than the transverse."

He will write that "few men have resolution
to . . . look over into the abyss." He fell
    on his hands and knees at the edge.
Intolerable! he cried, his head cloven
    by a savage migraine . . .

    Back at his desk, he writes
of "so beautiful an arch, so elevated, so light,
    and springing
        as it were up to heaven."

He likes the word "sublime."
But he can't get out of his head
the creeping and peeping.

    Mr. Jefferson writes through the night.

Artificer

Summer Solstice, Richmond, 2012

The boy has never heard the word *Confederacy,*
or *nigger,* thank God, spoken by a white man.
His parents frown when I mention Uncle Remus,
their eyes blank when I say, *Atlanta boys need to know
about the Tar Baby, the Briar Patch.* In all the nights
of bedtime stories in the guestroom dark,
his head on my shoulder, I've never told him
about my Golden Books, about Little Black Sambo,
his glorious outfit, his tiger peril, his Babel Tower
of pancakes. *Tubesock,* I call the boy these days,
though he can put away a respectable stack
at Aunt Sarah's, and two eggs over easy, four strips
of bacon, a bowl of oatmeal we call Muscle Mush.

Each morning I drop him at Tredegar
at a summer camp called *Passages* overrun
with kids of every kind. There's a sleek, black
Brooke gun out front. He walks to Belle Isle
under Jeff Davis Highway, on a bridge Grant's
engineers would have found worth some study.
I've shown him the Confederate Pyramid, Lee's
statue facing south, Stonewall's facing north,
JEB Stuart's corny getup. He's not afraid of
cliff heights or river depths. He likes the cannon
all over town. He knows I grew up in Savannah,
Abe's Christmas present from that brilliant
bastard Sherman. (*You want him to carry
that home?* his grandmother whispers.)

The Space Pak we've crammed into this old house
roars. Heat index 104 today. He'll come home wobbly,
eyes loose in his head, knobby knees unsteady,
licking his chapped lips. Still, he'll want me to drive
him back down Monument in the golden light.
You want to see the losers and traitors again?
Yeah, he says. *I like them. I think you mean Yes, sir,*

I say, and he Yes sirs me with a tiny wince.
What about Arthur Ashe? I say. *Well, he doesn't*
have a horse or a whole planet about to roll off
and crush his head. Good point, I say,
and off we go.

        Standing in front of the oldest wall
in town, I tell him about Poe, born within a month
of Lincoln, who marched Lafayette here at roughly
his age and turned out to be a pretty good soldier,
that Whitman's buddy Pete joined the Fayette
Artillery eight days after Virginia seceded.
I explain what a limerick is. I teach him the word
Artificer. Imagine, I say, *Poe might have been Commander*
of Artillery, maybe the guy who blows up bridges
after the rebels cross. What, my wife asks, *are you*
trying to do? Teach the boy some history, I say,
he lives in an eternal present. Good for him, she says,
and snaps off the light. *Artificer,* I say,
as I drift off, *Artificer, yes, good for him.*

Angelus: Chesapeake Bay

This is where the creek empties,
    where the speck spook
in the eelgrass. I'm no
       fisherman and everybody
    knows it.
          Heavy line, light
lure—how much of my life
      does *that* sum up?
         Shuffle and shoal
in the purblind glare. We haul in
     rocks and reds—or they do, mostly.
The air's thick with salt and funk.
        Hot, I say.
The captain's grave eyes . . .
      It's five years now. I'm still out there,
a seagull, hovering angel watching them
      reeling me in.

Vandalism of the Library Door

Someone's clawed through the beige
    slapped thick by men with sandwiches
in their speckled hands, men already turning
    to a hundred other doors. Someone stopped
    in a cliché of rage, found the fir green
that was here last term, olive before that,
    last decade's brown, then *orange!*
then original factory gray.

                And went deeper.
Inside the ravage of the bubbled paint the cuts
    are silver, gleaming and delicate, fine
    as spider webs, as glial cells, where
the raw metal shines. He must have brought
    his stylus down in a fist like a knife in the back,
    at first. And then the sweep from side to side,
the gouge here, and this final twist
    in the corner, as if to sign.

             And then I come
    and find in it design, assume he knew
the numbness of this beige, hope he felt the years
    in the colors he revealed. We can teach him
    Pollock, we always quip.
Up side his head. He's on my list. I'll phone the shop
    right now to have this work concealed.

That Coach in My Head Never Stops Asking
How Much I Want It

This shot that arcs
                toward my goddaughters' seven-foot basket
means nothing tonight. No, really.
                The time-thickened quarterback
                whose ass I saved from the Jenkins blitz twenty-
                five years ago will horse me here on the dark
driveway where we have strained
                our hook shots, hotdogged away our leads to keep
the tension low in what has become a belching
                two out of three after tacos and enough Sangria
                to change my depth perception
for a full working day.

                                        The set shot
upon which so much manhood once depended
                means nothing to me now as that ball goes,
I think, long, half-moon in the porch light
                streaming where our wives sit in the yellow glare
                drinking yet another nightcap. They have given up
or forgotten the wheel of the stars, forgotten that the girls, hypnotized blue
                in the x-ray of a film they should never see,
have school, that we've all got to push on to bed. It won't matter

if it's as long as it felt leaving these fingertips, more
                sweat in my eyes than I have earned with a limping layup,
a nailed-down jumper, and that flat set shot that will vanish,
                I know it, right past the pale backboard into the dark
                backyard where sprinklers shush the shadows
like a mother calming a child so tired he cannot surrender
                his whining to those ordinary dreams which are all, just now,
                he really needs.

Apocalypse

The surgeon, before he uncovered
the boy on the table, said *Well, what
have you done to yourself?* lifted the towel

the mother had placed so carefully, and actually
shouted *Good God!* (The kid's color was fine,
his shoulders and neck thick with muscle,

but there was his huge ass gouged and shredded—
exploded he told his wife—all three glutes,
and deep in the debris, exposed, the gleaming

nerve kinked, twisted.) By now, the father
frowned at his side, the one who'd turned
nineteen on Guadalcanal, the one who said

it was the worst wound he'd ever witnessed
on a living human. Even the nurses in the ER
had seen the boy signing a big-time football

contract on the local news, a hometown angel.
And, it was gone, the trip north, the college degree.
He didn't know this would set him free,

a stowaway through the Panama Canal,
that he'd sip hours of sacramental psychosis
from a tisane mixed by a child in Nishisonogi,

that he'd climb slowly to the Parthenon clothed in light,
limp down Fishamble Street, Handel's *Messiah*
surging through his head. The surgeon,

one of a set of rather famous twin docs,
would be dead three years later, victim
of a random infection. The boy's family gave up

the Methodist Church, its *Hymns for Times
of Trouble and Persecution.* And here was
the wonder of it on that sunlit afternoon:

There was no pain and only a little blood
as he stood in the yard across from his own
front door, the cars nose to nose in the street

going white, everything white as lambswool
for just a moment . . . Even then he didn't go down,
stood wondering why they were looking at him

like that, why his excitable mother was so
calm, barely touching his arm, then someone
holding him up as she drove the family Chevy

onto the neighbor's inviolable grass
and someone opened the car's back door
and someone else whispered *Can you take*

one step? And, you know, he could.

Erice

tucked up in the western sky—
Eryx tranquilized,
spayed, forgotten, cold clouds
moving through her
empty streets like ghosts—no,
ghosts of ghosts

Barelli Calls

When it rings, the phone
        I forgot to turn off, I might
as well answer it—that delicate
           metaphor, that gauzy scrim
of innuendo that married the world
    to the spirit yet somehow kept them
separate, that draped the one in the merely
             glittering other—
        it's gone.

Yo, Smitty, I hear you got a book coming out.
I can feel that forearm. Blocking Barelli
was like blocking a tree trunk or an anvil.
My neck begins to ache. God, it's great
to hear that mob movie accent I haven't
heard in years. Barelli, next to me on the bus
from the Hattiesburg airport to the hotel:
Smitty, what's that fucking stuff in the trees?
You're kidding, right? But Barelli's cartoon
consternation's perfectly genuine. *Spanish
moss? Jesus, that's gross!*

            Today, he claims
to remember a pig on a porch outside the airport
but doesn't remember when I asked him about
pickpockets in the Bronx. *Pickpockets?* he said.
*No, Smitty. Guys just hit you over the head
with a pipe and take their time. Pickpockets?
That's British, I think.*

            A surgeon wanted to cut
his shoulder. *Tell me, Doc,* he said, *if this was your
shoulder, would you do that? No, Doc, that hesitation's
just a little too long, thanks. Smitty, I could have
thrown the guy up the wall, so, yeah, I'm OK
after all these years, no complaints.*

We talk for hours, Delores looking in
from time to time, whispering *Dinner?*

. . . So, I wanted to tell ya, I'm bodyguarding
Ted Williams, you know, before he got sick,
and we're sitting there at lunch and he's such
a nice guy, always a gentleman with me and
his son's right there and I say, You know, Ted,
it's amazing, he looks just like you. And
Ted leans back and says, Yeah, but he can't
play baseball for shit.

Edgar Athletic Poe

He would have preferred that middle moniker,
    hated Allan, name and nemesis, and saw
himyoungself Byronic, sardonic, satiric, imperial, no
        less aquatic, who growing up barely
    in Richmond fought the tide
        from Mayo's Bridge to Warwick Bar,
emerging from the summer flood blistered heroic
    on face and shoulder.

Sometimes generous, typically mercurial, generally
    admired, perceptibly unleaderly, one May morning
        elected by the boys champion
in an arcing sprint round Mr. Jefferson's capitol columns.
        Headmaster Clarke kicked bright dust all the way
    back to class, muttering Latin . . .
Slight vertically and horizontally, but well-made, sinewy, active,

graceful, daring, in sport he was *facile princeps*,
        swift of unclubbed foot, elastic leaper high
and far, most enduring swimmer, and, O so rare, boxer ex-
    traordinaire, older than the others, having crossed
the ocean, gotten both ahead and behind,
        the plucky orphan, so refined,
    allowed his skull alarming pummeling, then
table-turning, swarmed one Selden, lumbering, winded, stung

wincing round the dooryard, artfully peppered and salted,
    the big man uncled. Poe declaimed a little Horace,
walked home alone, home to wealthy, stingy, phil-
        andering Allan and dying, always dying Fanny,
    languishing for love, who'd run her fingers through
the boy's poetic hair, search for his famous mother there
        in those gray eyes where Allan saw only

the poisonous fog of Russell Square, where the Englished child
    had first thinned to a razor. It was all downhill

into impoverished adulthood when Allan
yanked the orphan for gambling with gentlemen.
The boy who'd esteemed a proper fight, leap, run, swim had to claw
his way to a decent dinner, decent family, rep
as a man with a brilliant brain as well as the body
nature somehow lent him. The record shows

some shameful Northern scuffles, nothing Queensbury
or remotely cricket. Midway
through a decade of drudgery, dogfights, dunning, despair,
in Fordham he laughing split his trousers
leapfrogging with Sissy on a picnic perfect day. After she died
there was one last long jump, a challenge
Poe issued on a woodland stroll. He bested them all

but broke his good mood along with his gaiters,
"long worn and carefully kept." Barefoot, he limped back
to the cottage where Muddy nearly wept. But
he'd turned over a new alcohol leaf, so maybe,
she supposed, he could sell a little
metrical grief for a new pair of shoes.

Forum Boarium

... a civilized society is one exhibiting the five qualities of truth, beauty,
adventure, art, peace.
—Alfred North Whitehead

North Korea Puts Nuclear Threats on Hold in Favor of Business, Skiing and
Mushrooms
—*New York Times* headline

Romans roar through
    on their way to the beach.
As always, Asians line up to get their hands bitten off
        by an ancient manhole cover
    they saw in a movie.
        I'm on the hot seat (travertine), where
the sweet fountain water's cool from a Coke can.

    Oleanders and parasols, sulfur and asphalt,
a wheezing bus, a Vespa chafing at the crosswalk ...

        The Temple of Hercules Victor explodes
with sunlight, Hercules Olivarius, choose your poison.
    In the summer it hurts to look at it.
            I'm guessing Mussolini
    squashed that Coolie hat on it.
    How can they stand the heat, stand the line, stand
        so patiently with their little paper fans?
The one Caucasian couple quarrels and whines.

    And the Mouth of Truth? Nothing but a shadow
        behind its black bars.

Cut off from the river by the angry traffic: Hercules,
        indeed, oldest marble building in Rome,
    capitals luxurious with acanthus, a gift
of Lucius Mummius, who went at Corinth like
    a sponge on a stick, wiped the isthmus

clean of its stinking Greeks.
Did he know Sparta had refused Corinthian
demands to raze Athens
three hundred years before?

I find no record
of a Mummius sense of justice. Or humor.

These twenty Corinthian capitals—and every man in Corinth
beheaded. To Mummius, it was, as we say, bidness.
He thought the loot could be replaced
if the ships went down.
That Philistine Mummius Hell-

enizing Rome . . . So much irony, so little time. Imagine
Japan, China, Korea, the whole
whopping East
one-handed at its keyboards in the fall!
Last summer on the Corso: a beggar with no hands at all . . .
Speak, O, Bocca della Verità! Tell us that

Caca lives yet! The sun's her hydrogen bomb!
Non licet omnibus adire Corinthum!

After Church

Byrd Park, warm November

Little trees by the road: candleflames . . .
    and the ducks on the pond a net
that flings itself white and black, veering
    and skidding finally onto
        the sky . . .
            The fishermen cast,
the turtles sun in the eternal sun.
            Every squirrel has an acorn in its mouth.
A child is chasing a chicken . . .

And, oh, *that* tree! apple-green-incandescent!
            giant trunk twisting like a waterspout!
    The bigleafed fellow beside him runs in yellow fire
            down to the scummy canal . . .
    So why is the red maple
bright yellow, the japanese maple a dapple
        of feathery pink, red, green?
    God knows, God knows . . . The maidenhair tree
hasn't turned yet (ginko biloba)

        and doesn't stink today
        the way it did three weeks ago.
    Sweet gum's hung like Christmas
            with thousands of spiked balls . . .
    The maples light all the shadows.
        Cucumber magnolia, fifteen feet around—bare,
            its suckers harping the breeze.
Bare river birch, your tiny twigs dendrite the blue,
        don't they? Let's say so.

        Look!
    The Authorities have switched on
the cascade! And its
        double rainbow! God
    will not destroy us today
        by water.

Boot Hill & the Alimentary Spirit World
of Southern Joy

Are you dead? Are you skinny? Are you still
   the happiest girl in Chatham County? I'm there,
Billie, at the Clanton brothers' graves.
     I've just fired up the queasy family tract
       with a noon train of Old Hickory. I throw a rock
at some by-God purple mountains, worn down cowboy backdrops
no more majestic than old chaps. In other words, perfect.
     The rock doesn't travel far, but falls,
anyhow, into some real sagebrush.

      A few white crosses on a rocky hillside and I'm
so happy you'd think I was nine again,
     chunking dirt clobbers from behind your hedge
on Highway 80, just as pleased to see through the gap
        dusty cars as the Indians we said they were,
    braves Steve McQueen, smiling, puffed away
with dynamite sticks. The cars had plates from the West,
    that might as well have been the moon, desert landscapes
where all death was movie death. Something real
     seared into us in that sticky dark
where the bandit kept a squaw's head
    in a sack, meat to keep himself alive
     over the Sierras. How happy everything made you!

You laughed and Robby lost his Paydays and Pepsis
right between his knees. And you remember laughing so hard
     at Grandma's throwup on the kitchen floor
    that your tears mixed with the black bile stew
and rice and the undeniable corn?
    You watched Apache eat the same Alpo
twice and never gagged once. Don't look like horseflesh,
you said.

What goes in, comes out, your mama said. Unless, we knew
even then, it's transformed by the tunnel of time, unless
     it's taken up in all its fleshness, pumped

God knows how into the bloodstream of spirit
that can make Jesus shine like the Apocalypse
even on velvet blacker
than the symptom stool. All right: I never try
to see you when I'm home, never saw you once after
you grew breasts, washed those dirty pig tails,
combed them out.
Never tried to save you
from the grease-monkey husband that gave you twins
and broke your jaw, I hear, and would've killed you
if you hadn't chased him off
with his own twelve gauge. Or the Cuban carpenter
that nearly won you with his Spanish.
So I'm late. But I've brung you here,
thirty photogenic miles from Mexico, where it's 119 today,
hotter than records say ever was
a Meldrim summer
when we reeled squinting down sugardirt roads,
air floating thick as angels and I thought
I'd suffocate from heat and boredom till you
pulled me to the ditch and the frog sloshed
in the old tire and slimy glory was on me
again and I knew you'd never get old or die.

I'm here to tell you, girl, it's true:
you've been swallowed by the celluloid maw of time
where your bones are pickled flexible and wrapped in fat
and your eyes still half into laughter and fill when
a long-dead grandmother heaves and staggers from the room
she keeps so clean
you can eat off the floor.
This place ain't like Georgia at all. Here, everything
dries up and blows away. Genuine desert
out there, all the way to the mountains. I know

you're not you anymore and wouldn't get what the hell
    I'm talking about.
        I don't want you to call me—or even to write.
        I want you to wait for me back there
where I've put you, indigestible, translated,
                    fully spiritflesh forever.

The Old Crabber Has Gone Deaf

Oboe ghost sounds on the sea:
    milk globes less than moonbeams
flare green when he lifts his traps
      then fall shrill to strings.

His eyes have drowned
the tide's old grumble,
have brought pure sounds
out of the cranky waves,
sounds leaked in, somehow,
through the scratch of the old Philco,
through ears that never listened,
into the mesh of this rusty head.
Light sings to him now
like nobody ever did before.
Bell of moon on the water,
tinkle of stars on a heave of dark.

    A crab goes by, sideways,
  flat hands shushing
      the flashlight's clang.

He traps each blue crab
with its hunger,
still hums it toward
the uniform transformation
to orange.
But he won't eat
his catch anymore, is tired
of the crunch his thumbs hear
in the claw.

    In yellow buzzes of kitchen light
      beautiful women sit with sore fingers
  all along the bay.

Eternal

Keats and Severn by the Lateran backdoor,
    came to Rome in several senses
poor. The basket with its own little stove
    and its wretched stew the poet threw
onto the stones next to the charming sinking boat.

He was done with rhyme, he felt it
    from the first. There was shit
everywhere—in vicoli, in the fountains—humans shit
    wherever they pleased
in the Eternally Shitty City. Like ancient
    politicians showing battle scars, beggars displayed
deformities, running sores, blackened Byronic soles.

Coughing Keats, at the Casino Borghese, says
Napoleon's sister is in "beautiful bad taste." He looks
    and looks at her heavy feet, the lovely dent
they make in the sensuous stone. And in the flesh
    the old girl's full of leers these days
        for the Royal Engineers. How odd

his disgust, his need to avoid her or, not odd at all,
    his own flesh withering on the bone . . .
All those ousted princes dissipating along the Corso,
    crumbling like columns all over the Italy that's not
        Italy yet, sad-eyed, impotent royals,
glittering, drunk.

        Torlonia leans over the poet's papers,
    makes an offer and another that Severn knows
won't wash. He gathers his friend's drafts,
    bows what is not a bow exactly and goes,
Torlonia gazing after like a man who sees
    something he won't speak of, won't want
to remember. Too poetic, Keats says to Severn. What?
    The naked Paulina, the poet whispers, too

young, too beautiful. Canova's left out the rot, the
sweetness on the verge of nausea.
                              Severn bathes his brow,
tries to remember what to jot down, what

        to embalm. Rich, but not lush, Keats murmurs,
        but doesn't really, never did.
                              Madame Mere insists
on seeing visions—that boy, Keats was it?
        An eagle now, lifting her son into the sky
        from whence would come French domination,
                gleaming towers, cities reassembling

stone upon stone, the whole world happy
                and subdued. Why would a dead poet
        carry her dreadful son out of exile? The ways
                of the world are strange, she says,
wrinkles radiating like joy
                around her desperate eyes.

"A foolish moon in a foolish sky,"

my friend said to me, in English,
translating, she said, Pushkin.
It was a stage-set moon in a silver haze
over the apartment blocks. We turned
our backs on the crumbling flying saucer
of the metro station and walked into air
colder than any that had visited Savannah
since the Ice Age, into a little stand of woods
she called "a forest," the white path
slicked by schoolboys.

                    When I fell down
I was laughing that I was in Russia and
exactly the age Lenin had been
at Finland Station and lucky to fall
under the moon and rise without pain
and go on walking toward the little flat
where another "dinner" of beets and
dumplings would be steaming and tea
and *Gone With the Wind* would again be
playing in garish TV color and Clark Gable,
spitting image of my father at twenty-five,
speaking Russian and I have just been born
into a Cold War that will vanish one day
when he is old and I am no longer really young.

The Birth of Modern Poetry

Chucked out of the Academy,
      he sails straight
    to a pastry shop
        where the darkness laps
      the gossip in his head,
the whispers. That line
    lashed to that gondola:
        how it goes slack, goes taut.
"Suffering

      exists in order
        to make people think,"
    he will tell the daughter
    he can't yet imagine and certainly
does not want. Does he know
      what he wants? A good pasta and something
    potable. Liquid darkness and sputtering tapers—
      flickers—but, sometimes
        hard as gems . . .

You can spend an evening
      in the mask shop
    filling in
those empty eyes. Who really cares
      if he sinks or swims? Homer

    and Isabel. Hilda and Bill. He eats, when he eats,
too fast. The knife's silver edge: the grinding: that Yeats
    he reads and reads: he'll get
    to goddamn London and change the world.
      Which way to change it? How do you know?
    You make it new, make it up as you go,
      and you keep on moving.

Jacob, Swinging

Acne, flakes in his ears,
eyes dead green,
blond hair
brown with grease,
he'd go jitter and eyeroll
in the hotdog line
(and you'd think Elvis) then
just before elbow
or skull thumped on the tile,
you remembered.

Don't let him bite his tongue!
the crowd of faces spasmed
(as if he might want
to speak one day,
and if he couldn't
everything would die)
but he never used his tongue, even for that,
whether you jammed a spoon chattering
between the mucid teeth
or not.

And after he showed you
the whites of his eyes,
the height of his spine's arch,
something smoothed him out
(like the crumpled poem retrieved
from the corner of your room, poem
you remember like yesterday to a girl you can't)
and he rose in a crooked smile,
a performance of fidgets,
eyes loose in his head
like dice.

He never had to climb
those thick ropes that took you

breathless to the beams so high
above the circles on the hardwood floor.
(You hung there, trembling, hoping at least
your burning biceps could be seen
by all those upturned eyes. Someone held
the rope, someone climbed, that's the way
it was done, always.)
They're not for swinging! Coach bellowed
if you did.

But Coach froze with the rest
at the panic bar on the way to lunch
when Jacob (country aunt odor) squeezed past
into the dank cool
you assumed he would never know,
and ran and swung high and higher,
green eyes wide, loafers kicking
at the cinder block walls, an arc
through squares
of the high windows' light,
and never, somehow, never
letting go.

Cairbre & Bres the Beautiful

She'd had a long day, was sick
of the figures and the phone calls.
Tell me a story, she said.

                      "Bres the Beautiful,"
    I said, "taxed them into poverty, into
misery. Nobles chopped wood, built stone walls.
              Aristocratic hands blistered and calloused.
A cold rain lashed Tara. The poets refused to sing."

    "I need a drink," she said and I got her one.

"Cairbre stared at three dry cakes
      on a cracked plate. In verse he
cursed the king. The chieftans
        and their artisans shaped Nuada
a new arm, silver, joint to joint, sinew to sinew,
    with charred rushes to heal the old wound."
             She rubbed her knee,
    the one she had fallen on at the beach.
"Thus," I said, "the land was made whole again.
      Bres the Beautiful took fright, fled.

And then, guess what?" "And then," she said,
      yawning, "the poets sang."

The Good People

When we attack the earthworks, digging
    to get at the old gods inside, what, really,
        are we after? The silks and the silver,
the glory and the gold, tunics stitched
        with sky-thread, cheeks flushed
    as fuchia, pupils open as opium's
           portals? Is it love, finally, erect
with all that's proper, all that's possible? O
    the worm may sing like harps,
        reek like a hectare of roses—but
    first we thrust, we hack, right? Slashing
thorns, hardy, deep roots, stubborn, spilling, ripped out . . .

De Danaans, or Thank God for Plastic

She told me they came in a great fleet
　　　to steal the land from the Fir Bolgs,
that on the western strands they set fire
　　　　　　to their own boats. "No turning back,"
　　　she said, smirking—or maybe it was her version
of a leer. They believed the invaders
　　　　　had descended from a black cloud.
Out of the cloud they roared and the land
　　　bogged with blood. We were tossing back
　　　　　　Manhattans in the Shelbourne Hotel.
She'd said she wanted to interview me

　　　about "the litrachur of the American Sooth."
"At Tara their Lia Fail shrieked," she said,
　　　　　when their first king settled himself
　　　onto the stone. "Dagda's cauldron
　　　　　　　fed them all. Their spears
and their swords pierced even rocks." I said
　　　　　something about Faulkner, about
　　　Flannery getting the hell off the tracks.
　　　　　Nuada marched to Moytura and killed
Eochaid mac Eirc and his one hundred thousand . . .
　　　　　Survivors splashed away

　　　in all directions to tiny islands. She
offered me, I'm not making this up, her cherry.
　　　　　At Tara, the victors circled
　　　their shrieking stone, chanting
thanks, chanting imprecations. We
　　　shook hands on the sidewalk, dry hand,
firm, with tiny bones. She hadn't taken a single note.
　　　　　Maybe, I thought on my way down
Lower Baggott Street to sit beside snot-green Kavanagh
　　　and stare with him at the scummy canal, maybe
　　　　　she was wearing a wire.

Oh, *Duh!* to the Confederate Dead

It was evening. The room was cold
As a cliff of Norway; Uncle Bob's bullet hole
And the tasseling corn and Major Brogan's face
Above the fire in the half-light plainly said:
There's naught to talk to but the discomfited dead.
Being cold, I urged Lytle to the fire
In the blank twilight with not much left untold
By two old friends when both have published sixty years.
We unrolled the chill precision of metal chairs
And parked our carcasses in the smoky nil,
Gripped each a poker with his big big toe,
And stoked the fire's chipped music with implacable will.
There's precious little to do between day and dark,
Perhaps a quart or two of bourbon or some doggerel
Trotting with its magic bark
Or something as fine for the amenities,
Till dusk seals the windows, the fire grows bright,
And the wind saws the hill with a wedge of cheese.
We brooded awhile on angels and archfiends,
Heard the darkness grapple with the night
And give an old hag's commemorial sneeze
With her westward breast between her polar knees;
Then Lytle asked, "Which of us is dead?
Or even better: Who are the dead?"
And nothing more was said.
Ripped in the mansion's dark, we unclean shadows
Of the immoderate past squinted in the crumbling gloom
At the faint glow of Major Brogan's nose.
Then the window extended a fear to the room
Through the barbarous brine of booze in the blood
And suddenly I thought I heard the dark
Pounding its head on a rock, crying, "*Who are the dead?*!"
Then Lytle turned with an oath—and went to bed.

Coda alla Vaccinara

(Monte Testaccio)

From Keats's grave, past the Paladiana and Coyote
nightclubs, I limped to the celebrated
ristorante, determined to play it safe this year,
gout-wise, and eat only ox tail, where twelve
months ago I had the intestines and the tripe
and the sweet, sweet testicles and paid,
as they say, the price. I like to think
this is where Pope Leo enjoyed orange-
throwing contests, whatever they might
have been. But I *know* this is where, in his
God-has-given-us-the-papacy-let-us-enjoy-it
frame of mind, that jolly, genial, generous fellow
loved with a special relish the game of the rolling
of the barrels down ancient Rome's famous
trash heap.

       The poor and the country folk liked Leo,
though they kept their distance, partly because
of the odor of his anal fistula. His advisors
mouth-breathed at the side of His Obesity, who
trembled with delight. Machiavelli smiled
almost genuinely as Il Papa squealed
and pounded his palms.

       The barrels
gathered impressive speed clink-clanking down
one hundred and fifty feet of weed-sprouting

potsherds, amphorae so scrupulously broken, so
carefully stacked, convex into concave, century
after century, and the barrels out of the sky
making little landslides, small avalanches of
tumbling points and edges, and the people,
so *many* people, rushing to catch the pig-filled
barrels, risking some of their not-yet-ruined faces,
risking the crushed sternum and the splintered ribs,
shattered arms, legs smashed to pieces—
Can you imagine how they came hurtling
down that commerce-created mountain, that
monument to the discipline of year upon year
of oil and wine from all over the Mediterranean?
This was not the running of the bulls, fleeing
from frightened, hugely pissed off beasts. *This*
was more like the drunks at Daytona trying
to catch the cars as they roared around the track.

"Some fun!" said Flannery's Bobby Lee,
I thought, ungenerously. A mezzo of red
arrived and then my wife's exquisite liver
and my steaming ox tail, so fat-sweet, so lush
with perfect pomodori and sprinkles of cioccolato.
When a barrel broke open, the terrified pig lit out
for any space not filled with a hungry grin,
and the pope's litter, flush with his enormous
capacity for pleasure, rocked with, I suddenly
want to believe, a not-entirely-unwholesome
hilarity, with, let's say, a genuinely warm
fellow-feeling all the way back to the papal palace.

Monk & Mason

      Monk, taut,
thin as a cord, was my kind
of lineman that first year
I coached, slashing, all out
at all times. When I called him to me,
the caged face came in a satisfying
net of blood from the layered scar
that gritted the nose to the eyes.
Those eyes: wild and watery and black,
begging to please, to hurt.

      Mason
weighed ten pounds more, a paltry
one seventy-five, but drove me
up the wall in practice, too soft,
yielding, full of *yessir* but executing
always a kind of padded shrug.
Monk did what I told him, punished
the double-team in a whack and crackle
of plastic and bone. Mason, damn him,
muffled the blow, skated
into our baffled backers—or, true,
rode the offensive wave
to drag down somehow
a short gain, broke all the rules
and managed still to avoid
being blown away.

      Monk started
of course, butted the big boys
starry-eyed play after play, knifed
through the guard's outside gap,
stunned the halfback to attention
on the second step of a simple dive.
How could you not love him?
He knew the Slant and Loop

like the back of his broken hand,
took the proper angle on the sweep
and caught the runner cutting back
blind with thirty yards of terrible
momentum. You almost wanted
to look away.

Sometimes,
in the roil and confusion
of grunts and thuds, his side, the left,
The Slaughterhouse, would begin
to cough up turf. Buzzard Blitz,
Ugly Surprise, Noseguard To,
nothing worked. That's when Mason went in,
waddling past hunch-shouldered,
bleeding, limping, sweat-glazed Monk,
apologizing as he came,
sometimes crying.

It's OK,
I'd say, and wedge his hot neck
in the bend of my elbow. Side by side
we'd watch Mason's ducking dodge
throw off the blocker's rhythm.
It took me years to learn
what Mason wasn't trying
to teach anybody. Yearning,
tormented, and finally dead Monk
never did, belted at home
stiff in the air, hanging
tough three inches
from earth's ease, relief
the rest of us, no matter how mean,
took and took.

Out there beyond us,
the other guys' looming hulk
lunged at the ax blow that no longer fell,
missed the flicker of Mason, who held out
his hands as if to cast a spell,
about as solid as a dust web to one
who'd finally steeled himself
to hit back hard and now
had to learn to keep his head
out of the dirt long enough to shadow
this ghost of a lineman, this parody
who'd found a new way
to take all the fun out of the game.
When they finally got Mason's number,
I told Monk—fresh, whining to go—
to get back in there and do some damage.
His eyes always told me
he would.

John Smith in Virginia

In two hundred years it would become
    the island they were ordered to settle,
that deep-water peninsula swarming
        with death.

At Point Comfort they hailed,
thus christened, "The James!"

      Captain Newport's letters sing
the beauties and the bounties of this
    fair land, one-third
of the continent their Virginia, one-third
        of the men gentle, soft handed. And
    then there's this Smith, no
        gentleman, the Big Mouth
    their documents reveal
    as one of their leaders. Sheesh. He grins
like a wolf as they take off the shackles.

In Holland he'd fought the Spaniard,
    in Transylvania, the Turk (he said),
        had taken three turbaned heads
    and a coat of arms. At the Globe,
        Hamlet fretted about being,
while was Smith all over the globe
    furiously becoming. Tedious,
all that beheading, he yawns, then
    tells them of the Ottoman princess,
beautiful, of course, who had fallen
    for him and saved his
blah blah blah. Indian, Ottoman, severed heads,
    maidens—seen one, seen 'em all.

So, after five months Atlanticking, they
    chop pines, build huts, and, of course,
a church. This Smith, always shouting,

cursing, scribbling, boasting . . . Where is,
the men grumble, the gold?
             Newport sails blithely
away, two of three ships stuffed with sassafras
      for London's syphilis. (New World give it us,
New World damn well cure it, eh?)

A year later Newport finds thirty-eight souls,
             and those starving. "Let us pray," he says,
      and down go the skeletons on their swollen knees.
Indians, their only hope for help, attack. Newport
      sails away—so Smith gets down to work,
dickers with Powhatan, gets saved by
      a (yawn) princess not far from Richmond—
See the ghostly towers shimmering in the future!—
      disciplines the men
   to mutiny with six-hour shifts, this crowd
of Maynard G. Krebses shouting *Work?!*

Some grow callouses, all resentments.
They construct, let us say, our first (pitiful) Pentagon.

For their constant streams of glowing lies,
      Smith and Newport earn more and more
micromanagement: Find a northwest passage,
      find the Roanoke Islanders, find, by God,
   some gold. Oh, and put this crown on
             Powhatan's greasy head, wrap him
      in this scarlet cloak. Or, just
kill him and find another. And don't forget
      to convert the savages.
                   When someone tries
to blow off his balls, Smith sees his chance.
      Powder burns want London medicos,
he says and off, sarcastically, he sails.

Birds of the Air

Matthew 6:26

Mother slumps, both sides of her face regarding nothing.

Dad tells us what we already know:
gold finches have shimmered in that there holly,
those cat's whiskers have stopped going pink at sundown.

On the hill the sourwoods still won't relax.

Well, I say, we've got to go: Men in space suits
might close the beltway: Remember that blue scum
that kept us out of Baltimore once.

Maybe you are waiting for the trees to applaud the rain.

None of her plants can hack this drought, Dad says,
and her too crippled to look after them.
I'd call this a toad strangler, I say.

Nothing lasts, he says. This won't save a single dogwood.

I stare hard at you staring at Mother staring at nothing.
Make me the bad guy that thinks about time.
Gotta go, never can tell, this early bird's not so early.

Early bird, she says, early bird. But we're not sure.

Noseguard

My place is at the center;
my job, disorder.
I spit on their balls
between plays, I coil
on all fours at their stitches,
200 pounds of iron-sculpted flesh
on a hair trigger, famished
for the fumbled exchange,
the passing hand smashed
in a clash of helmets,
fighting to keep my face
aimed at the fullback's heart.

The growling stones
take their places between me
and a jittery boy
holding a football to his ear,
the stream I must swim against,
slam, pull, butt, spin,
and go down under three my size,
the ball gone, masks
like shrapnel in the legal backstab
of the passblock, clawing.
And again, and again, always
the glancing tackle, the whistle
too soon . . .

For others, the fear
of empty air,
naked to the isolating moment
of the bomb, long
strides in the open,
where contact is one
dreamlike explosion in the future,
at the end of the clear flight
of running . . .

For me, jammed space
in an avalanche
of helmets,
dust, the jumbled debris
of knees, of bodies writhing
on the earth, gnawed
cleats eye-high raking
on columns of leg, elbows
in the air like grenades.

After the horn,
in the stinging shower,
red seeps from a score of gouges,
and hearts throb all over my flesh.
They will bloom
the color of dirt.

I never see
the dark tunnels I move through
under the empty stands.
Always jammed in the head
the tailback stuck
in the sudden light
of the missed block,
paralyzed like a rabbit
waiting for the shotgun blast
of my caged face.

Just the Big Three

I.

Shower, I'm alone in the team shower.
Steam and silence.

The locker room is empty. I am dream
dressing. Music. In the gym?

Petula Clark is downtown.
I emerge into darkness blurring
with music and people dancing.

Oh, yeah, the sock hop.
I don't remember anything else.

Somebody told me I couldn't
get my shoulder pads off,

that Coach cut them off with scissors.

II.

That's my friend's face, what's
his name, laughing at me, he
looks so happy. Bobby, he says.
I'm Bobby? And he nearly goes
down laughing. *My girlfriend's
name is Bert?* Oh, my God,
he says, electric glee all over him.
I do know one thing, I say, and
now I'm laughing, too. *I weigh
one hundred and ninety-four pounds.*

They sent me to a doctor that time,
the *only* time in ten years—they sent

me to the local quack, the one who
had sewed a small turd of mud
into my ripped calf two years before.
They say I smiled all day, went
to bed chuckling.

III.

Again, hilarity, my friend in the helmet,
Jim, yes, Jim, All-American receiver, such
snickering and hooting and he says
we're both here on the bench, because.

We're way down the bench, away
from the coaches.

            Later, they tell me
I was grinning when they leaned down
to lift me. I was snuggling
the fifty yard line, the grass and the chalk.

Every other time, I was walking around,
zombie-style, upright. That was the *only* time,
I swear, that I was down and out.
Jesus. Karsarda said I had gone
for the kicker's knee just as he lifted it,
hard. *Did* he *go down?* Oh, hell, yeah, he said,
but he got right up.

Hurdling the Wedge

—Herman Melville

Did I tell you about the time
I tried to hurdle the wedge at VMI?
(Right, the wedge was legal back in those days
when helmet-to-helmet was simply a good hit
    and spearing was de rigueur.)

    Wedge-buster that I was,
I'd come down on the first kickoff to see what
looked like midgets—can you say midgets
any more?—well, midgets shoulder to shoulder
in that running crouch. Napalm and cluster bombs
had scared most students away from the
military schools. (Yes, players were actually
    students in those days.)

    After I had scattered them like duckpins
and missed the tackle, I decided to do something so
outrageous none of my buddies or coaches
would ever forget it. Next kickoff, came flying down,
faked a low dive at the point man's ankles, and threw
    my left leg straight over the guy's off shoulder,

    praying for a perfect hurdler's clearance.
Lord, wouldn't that've been something? Can't you see
the runner's eyes as I appear like whispering death
before him, a missile promising blank oblivion, hero
of a hundred film-session run-backs, the biggest
    hit, by God, in the history

    of kick coverage? Recently, while
getting my exercise with Wii bowling, I flashed back
to that moment, to that sweet anticipation, visualization
of the nearly supernatural. Oh, how I loved winging

down the field to the splendid explosion! Every time—
the raptor's rapture, an F4 Phantom's high-G thrill,
    closest I ever got to combat elation.

            What happened? Military midget
leaned down for the low shot, I got my leg just where
I wanted it, and then he did what I would have done—
arched his back and shot me high into the air. Went
up about twelve feet, felt like twenty. I reached
    for the runner as he went by

            far below. By the time I touched down
nobody was there. At the Sunday meeting, in the dark,
there were a couple of gasps. Then a gaggle of guffaws.
Coach Haupt said, "Smitty, I didn't know you could fly."
    (He did, though. And so did I.)

Maximus, Minimus

Jaundiced Clement conducted
the ceremony himself, joining
fourteen-year-old Caterina to
the third creation of the Duke
of Orléans, then shuffled off
to Rome to die—which great city
threw the party prodigious, one
Roman running a sword through
the dead pope's entrails, another
changing "Clemens Pontifax
Maximus" to "Inclemens Pontifex
Minimus." History is silent
about Caterina's grief, glee.
Only that liar Cellini claimed
to have wept, claimed to have
kissed the little yellow feet, cold
as St. Peter's. That is to say
Cambio's graceless St. Peter,
which you can still kiss today,
the one with the toes worn
smooth by the lips of the pious.

Seven Years After the Fall

Just Out of the Taxi from the Terminal

The Neva's a snowfield.
Headline: a bombing in Jerusalem
    near the main bus station. The poet Brodsky,
not a Russian? "No, no," says Oleg, "Israeli."
        My brain's a kind of slush, so it takes me
    awhile to get that: a Jew.
        Eight time zones away,
my wife's mother's intestines
        uncoil in the hands of a young surgeon.
The O.R.'s light is this
        pale northern glow.

Settling In

    I've got a pocket full
of rubles, and the Metro stations
        are named for poets. Still,
the ruble's nearly worthless, and the city's a
    nightmare version of Venice, canals
        all paved white, vistas,
    paralyzed, a boreal de Chirico.
The golden spike of the Admiralty middlefingers
    a lid of clouds. It's 23 Farengate,
Natalia says. What's that? I'll never
    write a single Russian stanza, but
        I sure wish I had Gogol's overcoat.
    And yours, too, buddy. I'd even wear Anna's
full-length fur, the blond one she claims
        is Australian possum.

Cityscape

The place is holding its breath. White colonnades
at attention inspect the pants properly tucked into my boots.
    Black smokestacks close in from the suburbs,
the Devil's troops coming to mock, then annihilate
    this classicism. Rumor has it
        the warehouses on the hooped horizon
are crammed with weapons shipped here for destruction
        after the fall of the USSR.
    Duma means thought, somebody said. Or thinking.
Duma, Duma, Duma, I say, on my way down
        Nevsky Prospekt.

The Locals

Graffiti in Svetlana's piss-stinking stairwell:
        "A lot of milk, / but no stomach. /
    "A brick, a head, / I want a cat."
Lumps of ice everywhere like varnished rocks.
        I fall down. I fall down again.
When mild, bald men put on
        their fur hats they become beasts,
    intimidating, some even demonic.
Hatless, they are affable, childlike, courteous.
    When you photograph people—when you ask
        if you can—it's no, no, no, no, but
not convincingly, and then you snap them and they say,
        Thank you.

Dostoevsky's Last Flat

Dmitri phones: Please come
on Saturday. Metro stop Dostoevsky,
     walk past Dostoevsky's last flat
on your right, on your left
    through the archway, then left into
       the courtyard, the door
    near the corner.
We are so sorry for the smell. Here,
    the hallway is part of the street,
       not like the U.S.

John Reed Street

When I got to Finland Station,
     I was 47, same age as Lenin.
    One thousand rubles were the same
as twenty cents. The Venice of the north
     was frozen, even the Russians
said it was cold. Natalia stifled a laugh
    when I fell on the ice, but she fell, too,
     before we reached
    John Reed Street.

Not There Yet

On a tiny, leaning bus,
we tour St. Petersburg, but the windows
are frosted and we can't see much. The guide
Englishes a mush of syllables. Then we eat beets,
Crimean peaches, some kernels called Greek nuts,
foul dumplings, shredded carrots. Vodka, then cognac.

I wake from dreamless sleep
in a freezing room. Out the window, far below: Desolation
of hardpacked snow. A bulky man
leads a boy by the hand
from nowhere to nowhere. Or maybe a girl.
They have no faces.

St. Petersburg, Petrograd, Leningrad, Petersburg

Oleg had white teeth, but Natalia's were golden.
He taught "navigation" at the Frunze, she, physics
at Public School 625. He said literature was "a drug,"
and she came shouting, red-faced from the kitchen.
Dima, twenty-two, drank vodka in the metro
on the way to morning class. He mocked the KGB
right there in the living room. I thought he would
cry when I gave him the carton of Marlboros.
Natalia began to look at me all the time, and Oleg
looked at her looking at me. At the celebration
of Women's Day, their friends, whose daughter was
still too alive to mention, looked away from Natalia
when she looked at me. They insisted I sit in the
cushioned chair. Had they visited the U.S.? The men
looked embarrassed, they looked like boys
when they said they had seen San Diego
through a periscope.

 Jay and Laura Mumble had
brought their children and their Mississippi vowels
to a place where the MacDonald's was full of Mafia.
I never saw them again after the airport. I don't
remember ever smelling the sea. I was cold the whole
time. There was a kind of patience in everybody's
unhappiness, in that transparent anxiety. I'll bet
they're all still waiting for the great change, still
glum and childlike, wrapped up against the cold,
pants legs tucked properly into their admirable boots.
I had no head for its abstraction, the city's design.
Half the time I couldn't see it at all. I couldn't think.
I was cold then colder. There wasn't enough bourbon.
Natalia insisted I squeeze ketchup on my noodles
with their hints of beef. One night she gave me
a larger glass for the Stolichnaya, but she and Oleg
drank from the same footed thimble. In the morning,

the mercury outside the kitchen window: minus 13
in the pearly glow. The only picture I'm sure I saw
in the Winter Palace: Rembrandt: Abraham's brutal hand
on the boy's face, the head back, the white neck . . .

Leningrad

Out of the depths the Party said would
save the faithful, I rolled on thunder

    toward the light of Leningrad
  amid a forest of silent
      colonels in their perfect
   uniforms. How long it took us

to reach the top! Then my Cold War nightmares
stepped toward the green shacks bejeweled

  with merchandise
      and it was not Leningrad,
    but Petersburg and they fanned out
  toward the cans marked "Gin"

and the bananas and backpacks hanging like traitors
in the March glare of a rare clear sky. "Pardon,"

   said the one I'd blocked, and the world
      was safe, reeling
   toward oblivion.

What's Wrong with the Baseball Hall of Fame

Every glove as clean as flesh can get.

Even Cobb's cleats, even Cobb's *teeth* sanitized
as if prepared to make their first uncorrupted wounds.

No sweat: the locker room where you sit waiting
for the movie that won't be even a movie but a slightness
you know will make you cry and angry that you cried:

*stink*less, that bright room, cool with the coolness
of endorsement heaven, no dank dimness
before warmup in the sweet, hot air, no cave
to drag your grittiness through to a hot trance of steam:

a waiting room wallpapered with unscuffed uniforms.

You look up toward some player's palaver:
cathode rays in a Janus box. Sure as hell,

there's Maris, dark circles under his eyes, wary, unsmiling,
as if he knows he's just an image, a ghost of an image.
He looks right at you, sullen, as if he knows

exactly where you are. As if he knows
where you're going next.

What's Right with the Baseball Hall of Fame

Not the bronzes, by God, Ted Williams's hat brim
all wrong on the left, lopsided, Mantle's teeth
ridiculously distinct, a mouth of singles.

The *fact* of the bronzes: Yes: That they are there.

That those numbers, some of them, change every Wednesday
on their black wall of oblivion. That Williams and the Babe,
supple in their burly primes, are made of wood, take swings
at each other in a room full of light. That a glass case of balls,
no more than three under any season, tells every itchy boy
you can pitch a no-hitter and still lose, like Harvey Haddix.

The Babe's big polo coat, the little model of the Polo Grounds,

Shoeless Joe's 1920 contract, signed in Savannah,
my hometown, where the first ball I ever tried to field in a game,
a little blooper foul, impersonated the sun and hit me
square in the forehead and made Sugar Bear, my coach, foreman
at the container plant, laugh till he fell off the bench. It hit me
right under the brim, smack in the frontal lobe
and made me smarter.

Thirteen Ways of Looking at Half-Rubber

I

Among twenty Georgia pastimes,
The only one that moves me now
Is the game of half-rubber.

II

You need three players only,
Each player a Trinity of skills,
Each player his own full team.

III

The dome zipped in the summer sun,
A blur—half there, half air.

IV

A pitcher and a catcher
Is catch.
A pitcher and a catcher and a batter
Is a tournament.

V

I do not know which to prefer,
The beauty of the sharp curve
Or the beauty of the quick riser,
The broomstick whistling
Or just after.

VI

Humidity filled the little yard
With barbaric yawps.
The shadow circle, oval
Crossed the grass, to and fro.

The mood
Traced in the shadow
Eternal youth.

VII

O bony boys of Chatham County,
Why do you imagine the major leagues?
Do you not see how this mezzo-marvel
Makes the gods pause
To look at you?

VIII

I know the oiled glove
And the joy of running bases;
But I know, too,
That the half-rubber is involved
In what I know.

IX

When he made that diving catch,
Stan became famous
To a small circle.

X

At the sight of Haskell's fastball
Flattening out,
Even Yankee scouts
Would cry out sharply.

XI

My father took a bus to Parris Island,
Sick of cropping tobacco.
Once, a fear pierced him,
In that he doubted
Half-rubbers ever flew
North of Georgia.

XII

The half-rubber is flying.
The war must be over.

XIII

It was game time all afternoon.
I was throwing
And I was going to throw.
My father caught
Everything I threw.

Brampton Road

A warm Heineken in each hand, I stood
    giggling with the girls across the ditch,
while he took his position
    out in front of the roaring Chevys,
        one in the driving lane, one in the passing,
fenders no more, I swear, than a yard apart.

    It was his idea and it didn't seem crazy, until
there he was, grinning in the glare, holding out his arms
    like Jesus—no, like he was on the court
guarding his man, knees bent, eyes narrow.
    All these years later, it's a Caravaggio:
        ultimate black, harrowing light.
Then his arms dropped and he vanished
        into a tunnel of squalling darkness.

I've told this rarely, every time stalling the conversation,
    always to bored, condescending eyes.
    Nothing, they imply correctly,
happened. Both cars fishtailed off the line
    and Danny was gone
    as they writhed on rubbersmoke then shot off
    toward we hoped nothing
coming in the other direction. And nothing was coming
    that night, no delayed lumber truck, no
Garden City cruiser, no belated buddies looking us up.
    The drivers, whoever they were, lived. My eyes

adjusted, conjured an upright Danny
    laughing toward me, that big hand out
    for his beer. Isn't this really the way
people change? I knew I'd never do it again, never

    again bear witness
to the senior class president, basketball captain
    rendering his own destruction. The fact that he's dead,

all these decades later, in his bed—husband,
father, grandfather, Chamber of Commerce, Citizen
    of the Year—what does that change? My wife says
        I'm risk-averse. It's not true.
It would have been a soft thump, I think,
        if the paint jobs had been saved
    by the perfect cushion

of pliable flesh. He's still curled up there
    on the center line, utterly still,
        no blood, no scuffs even, all
the damage deep inside. *I've got to study,* I used to say.
    It's late, I used to say,
Please take me home. My father's going to kill me.

Work: Savannah Roots

Except for the scrubbed month
    chilled in Mr. Dunham's tiled fluorescence
peddling spikes, bats, gloves,

it was ditch digging, old style, with shovel and pick.
    In the cut across the Esso slab
    after Melvin's jackhammer, the pair of us

    swung and jammed like Milledgeville crazies.
One hundred plus in the blinding Georgia sun
    would prove our manhood

single file behind men who'd been at it
    for decades putting food on tables.
    "You betta slow down," Louis said that first day,

    "you boys gonna fall out."
Royce sneered and swung the pick and I stomped
    the shovel with a football growl

and soon we were alone in the trench
    all of them knew wasn't safe anymore.
    Most days we laid conduit.

    For awhile we bailed a manhole
that filled back up every weekend. Ma Bell
    took us off that job after nearly a month

of nothing. I was five hundred miles north
    in Shakespeare when Earl died in the cave-in.
    Sam grabbed that live wire

    before Royce graduated. The rest of them
kept at it through hangovers
    and divorces, Friday night scraps,

short trips to the lockup. By August we were all
        slow and steady, sweat pouring off us
    like the promised waters

        of mercy as we hacked the black serpents
of the live oak roots. Earl sometimes
    keened a tune not quite gospel. Some days

we never lifted our eyes from the depths
        till the boss man said *Lunch* and the world
    came back—shady squares hung with moss,

        pines and palms and tarnished heroes
in uncool hats. "You Savannah boys now
    singed black as these nigras," one flabby foreman

hissed. Melvin's face was stone. Royce's
        deep tan burned. We dangled our boots
    in the slit, hip to hip for chow,

        sardines, pig's feet, pimento cheese, bruised
        apples out of paper bags, pretended
we'd all stay at it to the crack of doom,

        that some of us wouldn't go
off north to read a bunch of books. So much
    laughter! How did Sam finish

that story about the deaf girl
        and the donkey? Oh, each of us
    was clever in his own silly way, all of us

    sharing that huge swamp stink,
        and clowning like the Bard's gravediggers
in the heavy, sodden air.

1911

A stone fell from the sky into Egypt,
(killed a dog), Cubism into the language,
Madox Ford onto the floor, rolling . . .

Marinetti slapped a London gent
with a fine Italian glove.
Rome unveiled its wedding cake,

Richmond a school on Grove
for gentlemen, scholars.
Hundreds of words for snow

fell on the baffled Eskimo,
Edward Weston's Tropico stretched
under the palms, and Rorschach

smeared suggestive shapes we
all pretended not to see.
Tolstoy had his first year being

dead, Cavafy sailed off
in all directions, Yeats moved
upon the shadowy waters . . .

Hubert Humphrey saw the light,
Mahler, Gilbert, Pulitzer the dark,
George Moore lugged his crystal ideals

off to Cambridge . . . Portugal pulled
the plug on the One True Church, and
China killed already dead Confucius

just as FDR entered the NY Senate.
They just kept coming, trochees tumbling:
Ronald Regan, William Golding, bawling

babies, pure potential! Not to mention
a star fell in Egypt, killed a dog,
and the world began anew.

Winkles & Dillisk

Does he suspect the boys
      who sell him the tin cans, the cable,
the planks and nails, that they steal the stuff back
            at night then sell it again?
      He can wheelbarrow a load of bricks
all the way to the village—

and back, if he makes no sale.
      The old tar's been twisting ropes
         and rusty wire into varmints,
               into devils, into penises and breasts,
and something like pelvises, won't look you in the eye
      but sees you. You become a gargoyle

      you can recognize, if you will. Never talks
about the son lost at sea
         or the wife who died of lockjaw
               in his ropy arms,
told me the one thing he can't get
      out of his head is standing on a road

      somewhere between Longford and Sligo
watching the sun and the moon threaten each other
            on their opposite horizons.
      I, idiot, said,
"Silver apples of the moon, golden apples
      of the sun." He looked at me then,

      out of all those scorched wrinkles.
A colder blue you've never felt.
            And streaked, flecked, tainted.
      "Come on down to the shore," I said, "we
         can have some winkles and dillisk."
I was thinking of the cart run

by the saucy girl at the bottom
of the road, of her consoling eye.
"Shite," he said, "festering sea-wrack!
How 'bout a whiskey?" "Bit early for me,"
I said, but he was already moving,
going every which way in the joints
and disappearing fast.

What a Rush

to see you there in the sun, shining
with your best smile, not in fact
      gone forever, waving
off my question, delighted
    with my delight, sitting
bony on my lap, which you would never
      have done in life, my
proper friend, my neglected familiar.

So this is how it's going to be, this
    angry gratitude, this
      torment of the taken-
for-granted? Speak me a sonnet
    about Darwin and daguerreotypes
and this time I'll try not to wake
      to the raw dazzle of morning.

Virgin & Child with Monkey

(engraving by Albrecht Dürer, c. 1498)

I thought at first,
BVM, O Most Serene Madonna,
you were watching the child
who feeds the little bird
from the little sack.

But now I think you
watch below him, beyond him
the chained monkey
with the devil's face
who squats and looks me

square in the eye. I know you
will not lift your weepers to mine
no matter what I think
to ask or ask for.
Your maker's monogram lies

next to the monkey's tail and
wants also to mean *Anno Domini,*
the *D* beneath, inside
the *A* where it gives us
God, too, in the house

of the body. The black-faced
beast clearly likes me or wants to
bite a plug out of my flesh.
My vision flutters
back to you,

of course, your head
encircled by the white disk
erasing some of that
intriguing darkness
the sky offers.

The child leans out of your lap.
He will not fall. The child
feeds one who wants
to live in the air.
Across the river

(lake?) rises a half-
timbered structure, eccentric,
narrow, its proportions
roughly those of a man.
It points, let's say,

to Heaven. But the trees
sweep right to left in the wind
of your attention,
of the child's leaning,
of the water's

going away behind
the bird whose wing flares
but who stays
in the child's firm
grip above the whiplike

grasses and the brutal
stake and chain and the monkey
who won't stop
looking, who will never stop
looking at me.

Ultima Thule

Whither is fled the visionary gleam?
—*Wordsworth*

This, this is the end of earth. I am content.
—*John Quincy Adams*

Over roadkilled rabbits and blasted birds
big as turkeys, they hurried north over the Grampians,
dragging their troubles behind the Astra like tin cans
chasing cartoon newlyweds. The fax about their
friend's new cancer, the facts of their already
miserable marriage, intricate, inexplicable dreams
full of shame like influenza poisoning the body's
every interstice . . .
                         She always loved those words,
influenza, interstice. He said he couldn't get it out
of his head, that box of darkness always just
a few feet behind him. What did he want, eternal,
killing light?

And what did the world want to show them?
Swastikas on a monolith near Balmoral, leaden
wavelap at Loch Ness, ancient stone circles
shattered by apartment blocks, a swaying bridge
over a catastrophic gorge where they both
vomited their veggie burgers. *You must die
to live,* something whispered in the roadwhine,
You must die . . .
                         He was desperate to lodge
before nightfall, the rattling map disintegrating.

At last: Lochinver, target at the end of the *A*
as far out as seemed reasonable, on the map red
dead end in storms of ragged blue, in the windshield

a miniature Woodstock: babies in the street, pissers
in ponchos beside the macadam, cars and caravans,
tents and muck and picnics. No rooms, no rooms, no.
Hauching, he said, a word he'd just learned.
Cancha see? the red-faced woman said, *It's
the Highland Games. There's nothing between here
and Durness.*
            It's our honeymoon, she whispered,
covering the woman's beefy hand with her slender one.

In a misting rain they watched muscular men
toss a telephone pole not too far—till a fat fellow got it
to flip and the drenched crowd cheered. *The caber*,
he said, but she just looked at him. *Well, now, there's one
dear room, they tell me, at the Scourie Hotel. If you want it,
they'll hold it. Follow this road and you better go now.*

One black lane in the steady rain, shadowy fir forest
baffling the eye with identical treeshapes . . .

And so on to Scourie, not quite at the edge of creation.
Just inside the front door, on a sideboard: a little fish
in a flat pan, delicate spray of multicolored specks
along its stomach, exquisite ceramic, you'd swear,
with a sign pinned to it: "Woosey's breakfast."
Within an hour, a dozen more there in the foyer, all
brown trout laid out like treasures, every one pinned
with a man's name. The day ending, men leaned poles
rattling in the wall angle near the door. In the dark
paneled lobby they chalked today's loch, today's catch.
Low male voices, the click and scrape
of the blackboard.

                When all the light finally left the sky,
the whole world went blind. Now and then
a sheep bleated in the matchless silence.

This will give us, they said, better dreams.
Exercise tomorrow, jog or hike hard. Lotion
for the midges. We won't drive. We'll get
another good sleep before we go to see
what so horrified Dr. Johnson, before we go
to the very end. Every night they were strangers,
faceless couplers, smooth tangles, slick mouths
and moaning like singing, languid arias one
after another, one, then another one.

At breakfast the eyes were brazen or averted.

How could they have been fresh when they
traveled that narrow track through apocalyptic
glacial scour, not so much death's alluring
playground as a stone's unblinking stare
into the atheist sun? Did they find what
they came for? Is that what cured them?
Ultima Thule, was all they would say. Maybe
it was the thready waterfall the color of
their friend's thin hair, the deer grass,
sundew, butterwort here and there . . .

They declined a wrinkled sailor's offer
to get them round the rocks to Cape Wrath.
Each bought a hat that smelled like kerosene.
They said—and they said it together—
We have gone far enough. Then, they did
what most people do. They turned back.

Notes and Dedications

"A Dusting": Dedicated to Carole Weinstein.

"Bronze Boxer": In memory of Quent Alcorn.

"Mr. Jefferson Speaks of Rapture": Thanks to Lisa Spaar for commissioning this poem.

"Artificer": Dedicated to Russell Byrd Smith.

"Angelus: Chesapeake Bay": Dedicated to Don Johnson.

"Vandalism of the Library Door": Dedicated to Mary Horne.

"That Coach in My Head Never Stops Asking How Much I Want It": Dedicated to Stan Tretiak.

"Apocalypse": Dedicated to Rusty Wilson.

"Erice": In memory of Vickie Alley.

"Barelli Calls": Dedicated to John Barelli.

"Edgar Athletic Poe": Thanks to Arthur Hobson Quinn, Kenneth Silverman, Jeffrey Meyers, Daniel Hoffman, and most of Poe's many other biographers and commentators, nearly all of whom agree that young Poe was quite a good athlete. Dedicated to Charley Stillwell.

"Forum Boarium": Dedicated to Stephen Wood.

"After Church": Dedicated to Melissa Hollerith.

"Boot Hill & the Alimentary Spirit World of Southern Joy": In memory of Penny Austin.

"The Old Crabber Has Gone Deaf": Dedicated to George McVey.

"Eternal": Dedicated to Buffy Morgan.

"A foolish moon in a foolish sky," Dedicated to Natalia Makarovna.

"The Birth of Modern Poetry": Dedicated to Mary de Rachewiltz.

"Cairbre & Bres the Beautiful": Dedicated to Delores.

"The Good People": In memory of Seamus Heaney.

"Coda alla Vaccinara": Dedicated to Dave Cappella & Maria Frank.

"*Oh, Duh!* to the Confederate Dead": In memory of Andrew Lytle and Allen Tate. See Tate's "The Oath" as well as his "Death of Little Boys," "Ode to the Confederate Dead," "The Mediterranean," "The Swimmers," etc. Dedicated to T. R. Hummer.

"Monk & Mason": In memory of Brent Nunnery.

"John Smith in Virginia": Dedicated to Cliff Dickinson.

"Birds of the Air": In memory of Mamie Smith.

"Noseguard": Dedicated to coach Jack Miller and poet Dave Smith.

"Just the Big Three": In memory of Jack Higgs.

"Hurdling the Wedge": Dedicated to Joyce Duncan.

"Seven Years After the Fall": Dedicated to Joe Knox.

"Leningrad": Dedicated to Brad Whitehurst.

"What's Wrong with the Baseball Hall of Fame": Dedicated to Dick Crepeau.

"What's Right with the Baseball Hall of Fame": Dedicated to Tony Szymendera.

"Thirteen Ways of Looking at Half-Rubber": With, of course, apologies to Wallace Stevens. Dedicated to Dale Ritterbusch, Mark Noe, Scott Peterson, and Julie Tretiak, to all of whom the author introduced this splendid game. And in memory of J. K. Smith, who was a master half-rubber player. The piece more or less explains the game that originated in Savannah, Georgia, in the early twentieth century.

"Brampton Road": In memory of Danny Murray.

"1911": Dedicated to James Nalle Boyd.

"What a Rush": In memory of Claudia Emerson.

CPSIA information can be obtained
at www.ICGtesting.com
Printed in the USA
LVOW11s1742090817

544311LV00010B/132/P